LUNCHBOX

easy recipes • menus • shortcuts • practical ideas

PRO

Jenny Swann and Anne Prendergast

SOUTHGATE
PUBLISHERS

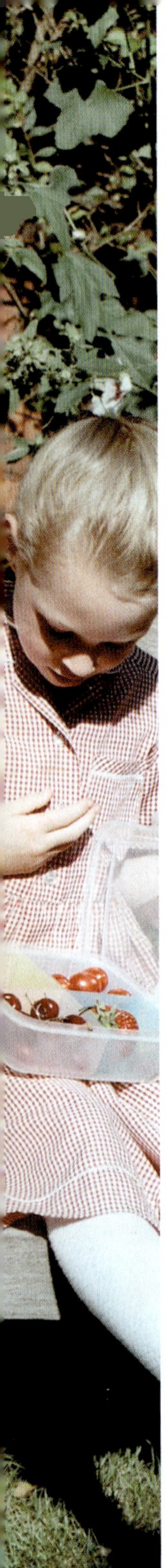

Copyright text © Jenny Swann and Anne Predergast 2005

Copyright photographs © see acknowledgements 2005

First published 2005 by Southgate Publishers Ltd

Southgate Publishers Ltd, The Square, Sandford, Crediton, Devon EX17 4LW

Printed and bound in Great Britain by Pensord Ltd, Blackwood, UK.

British Library Cataloguing in Publication Data

A CIP catalogue record for this book is available from the British Library.

ISBN 1–85741–195–1   ISBN 9781857411959

Acknowledgements

Text © Jenny Swann and Anne Prendergast

Photographs:
© Pat Collings (pps 4,7,9,24,27,28,29,30)
© John Walmsley, Education Photos (p12)
© Bubbles Photo Library (pps 3,5)
Front Cover and additional photos - Zara Media & Design Ltd, Drummond Johnstone

Thanks to everyone who offered expert help and advice, including: Ruth Stainer-Smith; Helen Buxton-Smith (Mid Devon PCT), Laura Warren (NCPTA); Pam Harvey (community nutritionist); Mandy Ross, Gillian Lam, Carol Atherton; Jess Sharp.

Thanks to the children involved in this book: Alice Harrison (front cover pic); Iseabail, Louis, Sam, Amelia and William; and our children: Carri, Emma, Lucy, Emily and Edward, who helped make the recipes and licked the spoons clean! Thanks also to Charlie, Harriet and Madeleine and Oliver for posing for photographs.

Thanks to Carri for the diagram on page 4.

Special thanks to Bernard and Peter for giving us the time and space to complete this book.

Contents

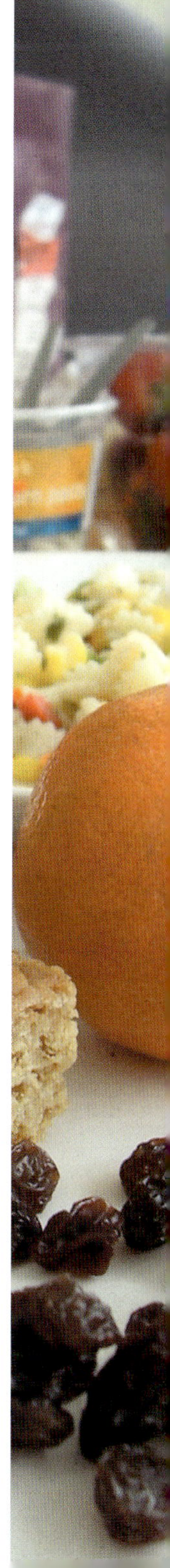

Introduction

Anyone who prepares lunchboxes each week will know that feeling on Sunday night, as they stare hopelessly into an almost empty fridge. We are two parents who want to take the work out of packed lunch planning and preparation. We've printed your shopping lists for you and compiled a four-week menu, aimed at primary school children though appealing also to older children. If you prefer a more relaxed approach we've included a pick and mix method. Of course the best part of this book is the range of delicious recipes that are easy, good value for money and healthy. Make your child's food look interesting and adapt our practical advice to your family's needs. Sunday night empty fridge experiences can become a thing of the past!

Lifelong habits and healthy eating

Your child's lunchbox is an important part of his or her future.

- Eating healthily in early life is likely to continue into adulthood.
- The number of obese children has more than doubled in twenty years. In 1998 the World Health Organisation designated obesity as a global epidemic.
- Overweight children are more likely to become overweight adults and may suffer physical and psychological problems.
- Anorexia nervosa and bulimia are among the most common chronic illnesses of adolescence. A balanced attitude to eating is important.
- Eating fruit and vegetables each day has many health benefits like reducing the risk of stroke, heart disease, and some forms of cancer.
- Remember that if your children are used to seeing you enjoy fruit and vegetables they probably will too.

As parents we know how difficult it can be finding a healthy way through the junk food which is heavily advertised, and seen as attractive by our children and their friends. Is it any wonder that we often take the easiest route and buy the foods which they think 'cool'? This book offers a realistic balance between their expectations and yours!

Talk to your child's school

It's a good idea to ask the school about lunch rules. Some schools ban certain foods. Sticking to the school rules helps keep the lunchtime a positive experience and doesn't single out your child as different.

You may want to consider the following:

- Does the school have any written guidelines?
- Will there be a member of staff to help unpack difficult packaging?
- Can the school warm up food? Or keep it chilled?
- Is there a policy of 'no sharing'? This is vital for children who have food allergies.
- Does the school provide a drink? Or cutlery?
- Where are the lunchboxes stored?
- Do the staff throw away uneaten lunchbox food at the end of lunchtime or does it come home to you so you can see what wasn't eaten? It's useful to know what your child didn't like.
- Does the school allow hot soup? Some schools may have health and safety concerns.

What is a balanced meal?

Sometimes the government guidelines about food choices are very dull and off-putting or very difficult to understand. We hear different things from different people and it's not easy to decide how to use the information. How can we work out the correct amounts of protein, fat, starch and sugar, let alone vitamins and minerals? And this is all extra work for us parents on top of the other things we are juggling with school aged children! Because of this we think it's best to relax and encourage your child to enjoy a wide variety of food.

Basically, food can be separated into the following categories:

Fruit and vegetables

We all need at least 5 portions of fruit and vegetables a day to stay healthy. Portions for young children can be smaller than the adult size of 80grams. Try and give plenty of variety; remember potatoes don`t count in this food group.

Bread, other cereals and potatoes.

Starchy foods from this group are the best food source of energy for everyone, young and old. Include more that are plain and not too fatty or sugary (e.g. jacket potatoes, pasta, low sugar cereals). Get your child used to some wholegrain varieties too (e.g. wholemeal or granary bread) - they are great for healthy insides.

Meat, fish and alternatives

Give children two or three helpings of meat, fish or eggs a day for growth. Include pulses eg beans and nuts as protein sources if your child is vegetarian. Try not to give too many processed foods from this group.

Foods containing fat / Foods and drinks containing sugar

Foods that are high in sugar should form a small part of the diet. Giving sugary foods and drinks between meals is harmful for teeth and these foods provide lots of calories without many other nutrients. Growing children should include some sources of fat in their diets, but it is better if this is provided mainly from the "Meat, fish and alternatives" and "Milk and dairy foods" groups rather than from too much fatty processed food (e.g. crisps, pastry).

Milk and dairy foods

Milk and dairy foods contain lots of calcium - very important for the development of strong bones and teeth. Try to include three helpings a day from this group. Low fat varieties have the same levels of calcium and are safe to give to children over the age of five.

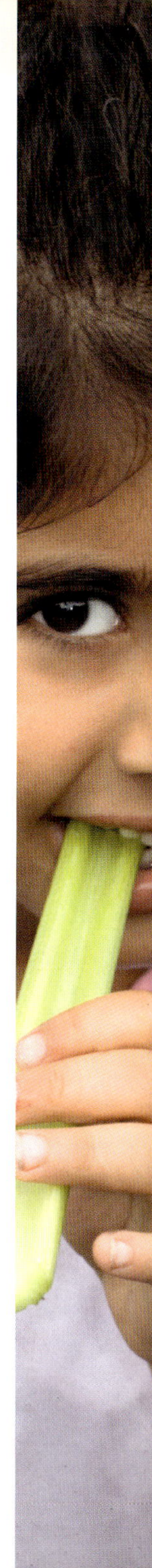

- Most school lunchboxes contain too much fat, salt and sugar, according to a recent government survey. The most popular foods were white bread sandwiches, crisps and a sweet 'dessert'.

- The current government recommendations are that a packed lunch should at least contain a portion of starch, protein and fruit or vegetables and ideally a dairy product too. See our pick and mix section on page 20.

- Try and find cunning ways of including food your child 'hates'. A fruit cake or a carrot cake may work where fresh fruit or carrot sticks do not. Encourage your child to try out new foods.

- It's not worth trying to be perfect. Allowing sugary snacks as treats is fine as part of a balanced eating plan. It's better to finish off a healthy lunch with a small treat than to snack between meals.

- You can go too far! At the extreme of healthy eating there is a condition called 'muesli malnutrition'. This is where children end up undernourished because their parents fill them up with too many high fibre foods which don't contain enough energy.

Children are far more likely to eat a healthy lunch if you involve them. They will enjoy helping you prepare their boxes and you will get to know their likes and dislikes. Presentation and packaging are important to children too - more of that later!

Food hygiene

Tummy upsets are often caused by mild food poisoning or lack of food hygiene. You can reduce the risk of this by:

- Washing your hands well before starting to prepare the lunchbox.
- Not using a chopping board that has been used to chop meat.
- Following manufacturers' freezing instructions carefully.
- Washing the lunchbox thoroughly each day.
- Reminding your children to wash their hands before meals.

It is important to keep food cool to avoid growth of bacteria, especially in the summer or in warm classrooms. Cold rice is notorious for causing tummy upsets so take care to rapidly cool cooked rice and keep it in a fridge. There are several ways to keep lunchbox food cool:

- Some small items can be frozen and then put into the lunchbox in the morning. They will gradually defrost and keep any surrounding food cool too. Remember that this will only work with small things - large items may not defrost in time for lunch!
- Adding ice-cubes to drinks will help to keep the lunchbox cool.
- Using a mini ice-pack.
- Buying an insulated lunchbox: these often have fitted ice-packs.

Shopping for equipment

You will need a lunchbox and, unless you opt for cartons of juice, a flask for drinks. You might decide to buy some purpose-made lunchbox tubs and compartmentalised pots. A number of retailers sell these.

Lunchboxes

There is a wide variety of lunchboxes on the market - involve your child in choosing as a favourite colour or cartoon character can get lunch off to a good start.

- Choose one that your child can open easily.
- Ask other parents which designs are best. Some lunchboxes, although they may look attractive, break if knocked about.
- Look into buying an insulated box, or small ice packs to help keep food cool until lunchtime.

Drinks flasks

Again, it is useful to compare notes with other parents. In particular, look for:

- A flask that is leak proof.
- A flask that is easy to open and close.
- Insulated flasks that keep hot soups warm as well as cold drinks cold. Think about getting a wide necked one that could be used for hot meals such as pasta or thick soups if your school allows this.

Some parents use small, empty plastic bottles, which are replaced when they start looking the worse for wear. This often proves popular with slightly older children, who feel quite 'cool' swigging from a bottle. The drawback is that such bottles are rather fiddly to clean. Many children like sports-top bottles like cyclists use.

Other items

The following items are useful to have to hand:

- Paper napkins or kitchen roll, which is cheaper and works just as well.
- Plastic cutlery to avoid losing your main set piece by piece.
- Sandwich bags. You don't have to spend extra money on sandwich bags. How about recycling empty margarine tubs and other packaging that you can then use to put sandwiches in? If you want a professionally presented sandwich think about buying disposable sandwich packs from kitchenware specialists.
- Coloured stickers to write messages on, or other packaging that your child will find attractive.

Pulling it all together

Now that you are set up with the 'hardware', what are you going to put in it? And how are you going to present your offerings? On the following pages you will find some menu suggestions that are healthy, but realistic about what children will eat and enjoy.

As your children get older, they could put together their own lunchboxes, under your supervision. This will save time and help them understand how to prepare a balanced meal.

A note on sandwiches

- This favourite doesn't have to feature every day. However it can provide a nutritious and interesting lunch with some imagination.
- Try to steer away from white sliced bread. Many parents find that soft grain bread is a successful compromise for a child who isn't yet happy with wholemeal.
- Jazz up sandwiches by shaping them - into cars, animals or stars - with cutters. Even just using a large plastic tumbler as a cutter can be a quick and effective way of making them look more interesting.
- Pinwheel sandwiches are very popular with younger children. Get your child to roll out a slice of bread with a rolling pin, until it is very thin. Now spread it with a filling such as peanut butter, marmite or mashed banana. Roll it up swiss-roll style and cut into sections.
- 'Pocket handkerchiefs' appeal to younger children. Use a filling such as one of those suggested above, and chop the sandwich into lots of little squares.

Store cupboard/freezer basics

It's a good idea to keep a ready supply of certain foods. Stock up with loaves of sliced bread, mini pitta breads, bread rolls, muffins (both bread-style and cake-style), tortilla wraps and bagels. You can freeze them until you need them. You should end up with quite a variety to choose from.

You can freeze tubes of fromage frais which can then be eaten frozen like a lolly or, if they have defrosted by lunchtime, sucked out of the tube.

Useful cupboard items include:

bread sticks	jars of redcurrant	oatcakes
pasta	jelly	cereal bars
rice	jars of pickle	mini chocolate
eggs	tomato puree	bars for occasional
tins of sweetcorn	marmite	treats
tins of beans	honey	
tins of tuna	peanut butter	
tins of fruit	dried fruit	
pitted olives	(e.g. raisins,	
jars of pesto	apricots, mangoes,	
	apple rings)	

Use of leftovers

Use leftover pasta, potatoes, couscous or rice (see section on food hygiene) for a salad the next day. Add small pieces of raw or tinned vegetables such as red peppers, cucumber, sweetcorn, tomatoes, olives, peas, green beans, carrots and spring onions, and pulses such as kidney beans. Try some cubes of mozzarella or feta cheese, or chunks of chicken or ham. Leftover roast vegetables - such as parsnips, carrots, onions and peppers - can make a delicious and wholesome salad eaten cold the next day, in their own sweet juices.

Drinks

- Just as with the food, it is important to make sure your child likes the drink you put in the lunchbox. Water is the most thirst quenching but some children object to plain water.
- Think about the drink you pack for your children or you could undo all your good work in planning healthy meals. Try to vary the drinks given during the week.
- Avoid sugary, fizzy or caffeinated drinks. Children often accept flavoured mineral water as an alternative to the high sugar varieties. You can make your own by diluting fruit squash with sparkling mineral water if the school allows it.
- Pure fruit juices can be diluted with water to reduce sugar and save money.
- Consider sending in milk but make sure it is kept cold in an insulated flask. You could even add some chocolate powder to the milk once in a while as a special milkshake - they will still get the goodness of the milk, however it is served.
- Fresh fruit smoothies are brilliant as they mix fruit and dairy products. Blend fruit of your choice with some natural yogurt and a little milk. Remember this will need to be kept cool. Smoothies are not particularly thirst quenching so pack some water too.

Presentation and packaging

The appearance of lunchbox food will either attract your children or put them off.

Packages of sandwiches can be made more appealing if you slap a sticker on them. You could also put a sticker on items of fruit or pots of salad. Make your own stickers with messages such as 'Eat me', 'Eat me first', 'I made this', or 'The Romans/Vikings/Elizabethans munched these'. Gold stars can be stuck on fruit and then on uniform once the fruit has been eaten. Use colourful party bags for loose finger foods like grapes, cubes of cheese or dried fruit and nut mixtures.

In the summer, you could put in a 'durable' flower or a stem of rosemary or lavender.

Another idea is to write a message to your child and put that in. Lunchboxes tend to get bashed around, so avoid fragile items as part of the packaging.

Special occasions

Why not celebrate festivals such as Christmas, Easter, Diwali, Eid and the Chinese and Jewish New Years by including festive food in the lunchbox? Hallowe'en half-apples (unpeeled with 'eyes and a mouth' cut into them with an apple-corer for a ghostly effect) can delight your child. Ask your child's school for ideas and information in this area and look at our suggestions below on page 19.

If your child's birthday falls on a school day, make a 'surprise' lunchbox and wrap the contents in easy-to-remove birthday paper. Put in a 'Happy Birthday' sticker or card.

Themed lunchboxes

You can link in with what your child is learning at school. For instance, if the class is studying the Romans, put something Italian in the lunchbox; if they are learning about the Victorians, how about surfing the web for Mrs Beeton's recipes?

Another idea is to use colours or shapes as the theme of the lunchbox: for example, the contents could all be red, yellow, round or square items. You and your child will probably be able to think of many others.

Four weeks of menus

Planning ahead will save time. If you don't have time to make up lunchboxes from scratch in the morning put together as much as possible the previous evening.

To make life easier we have compiled a four week menu with a shopping list for each week. You'll need to have the store cupboard basics and a freezer shelf of breads ready.

The menus have been designed to be quick and easy to eat so that your child can go out to play as quickly as possible! All the menus can be adapted to suit your own child. In particular, if your child has specific food allergies, some of the suggestions may not be suitable. If you are too short of time to follow the fruit suggestions below, just pop in an apple, banana or bunch of grapes. Extra recipes and ideas follow on page 23.

Soups provide a nutritious warm lunch especially on cold days. Check first with your child's school that they are happy for hot soup to be brought in. Make sure that the soup is 'drinking hot' rather than 'piping hot' to prevent burnt tongues and accidental scalds.

Your child will soon let you know their likes and dislikes and which items their friends have in their lunchboxes. You will learn together as you go along.

Week One

Carrots
Celery
Cherry tomatoes
Cucumber
Cress
Salad
Apples
Grapes
Kiwi
Pitted olives
Ham
Cheese
Chicken
Hummus
Vanilla or natural yogurt
Fruit bread
Flapjack
Carrot cake
Chocolate brownies -
   homemade or otherwise

Monday

- carrot and celery cut into sticks
- tortilla wrap with tuna and sweetcorn filling
- kiwi sliced in half (pack a teaspoon so that it can be eaten like a boiled egg).
- fruit bread

Tuesday

- pasta salad with pasta shapes, tomatoes, ham and pitted olives (add a little olive oil to the cooked pasta to prevent it sticking together).
- stewed apple - add some raisins if you like. This can be made the previous evening. Include a small pot of natural or vanilla yogurt to add if desired.
- flapjack

Wednesday

- cucumber sticks with a small pot of hummus as a dip
- pitta bread stuffed with ham, salad, cheese cubes
- pot of dried fruit - apricots, raisins, apples
- slice of carrot cake

Thursday

- cherry tomatoes
- egg and cress sandwich
- fruit salad - grapes, apples, kiwi (pack a teaspoon)
- cereal bar

Friday

- pitted olives
- soft brown roll with sliced chicken
- oatcakes with cheese and apple
- chocolate brownie (see page 24)

Week Two

Apples
Pears
Cherry tomatoes
Pineapple - fresh or tinned
Grapes
Cucumber
Salad
Melon
Baby carrots
Soup - tin or ingredients for
     homemade
Cheddar and mozzarella cheese
Sausages - cocktail or long
     thin ones that can be sliced
Fromage frais tubes
Vanilla or natural yogurt
Flapjacks
Muffins (cake-style)
     - often bite sized ones work
     best or homemade
Currant buns

Monday

- soup with soft bread roll - either homemade or tinned soup of your choice in an insulated flask. You can improve tinned soup by adding cooked pasta or pulses.
- cubes of cheese and pineapple
- flapjack

Tuesday

- bread roll filled with mozzarella cheese and tomato smeared with pesto
- fruit salad; pineapple, grapes and pear
- frozen fromage frais
- muffin (cake-style) (see page 25)

Wednesday

- cherry tomatoes
- pinwheel sandwich with peanut butter filling
- natural or vanilla yogurt with a fruit puree or honey
- currant bun

Thursday

- cucumber strips with natural yogurt
- pitta filled with cheese, salad, tomatoes
- pineapple and melon salad
- cereal bar

Friday

- baby carrots
- salad of cooked sausage, cherry tomatoes and cucumber with a bread roll
- stewed apple and pear plus natural yogurt if desired
- small chocolate bar

Week Three

Celery
Peas/mangetout
Grapes
Strawberries
Raspberries
Clementines
Apple
Lemon
Peppers - red, yellow, orange
Carrots
Pineapple - fresh or tinned
Tomatoes
Cream cheese
Cheddar cheese
Walnuts
Chicken
Natural yogurt
Fromage frais tubes
Mayonnaise, if you haven't any
Flapjack
Muffin (cake-style)
Fairy cakes

Monday

- celery spread with cream cheese
- sandwich with chicken and redcurrant jelly
- small container of drained, tinned fruit
- flapjack

Tuesday

- peas in pods if available or mangetout
- cream cheese pinwheel sandwich
- fruit salad; grapes, strawberries, raspberries or others of your choice - use whole fruits that will not discolour or a mix of fresh and dried fruit
- cereal bar

Wednesday

- strips of red, yellow and orange peppers
- chicken waldorf salad with bread roll (see page 24)
- dried apple rings with natural yogurt dip
- muffin (cake-style)

Thursday

- carrot and raisin salad
- bread roll with egg and tomato
- grapes and clementine segments
- flapjack

Friday

- cheese and pineapple cubes
- pitta filled with tuna and sweetcorn combined with a small amount of mayonnaise
- frozen fromage frais
- fairy cake

Week Four

Grapes
Cherry tomatoes
Pitted olives
Apples
Pears
Banana
Lemon
Carrot
Cucumber
Celery
Vegetables for roasting such as
   peppers, courgettes, tomatoes
Cheddar cheese
Feta/mozzarella cheese
   (optional)
Ham
Hummus
Fromage frais
Vanilla or natural yogurt
Cream cheese
Muffins (both cake and
   bread-style)
Fruit cake
Chopped nuts
Chocolate brownies
   - homemade or otherwise

Monday

- rice salad (see food hygiene, page 6) with roasted vegetables - whatever may be left over from the weekend or peppers, tomatoes, courgettes. Add some mozzarella or feta cheese if your child likes
- small container of drained, tinned peaches
- muffin (cake-style)

Tuesday

- pitted olives
- mini pizza - this can simply be made by halving a bread-style muffin, spreading it with tomato puree and topping it with, for example, ham and cheese. Pop it under the grill just to melt the cheese - delicious eaten cold
- slices of apple and pear brushed with lemon to prevent discolouration
- cereal bar

Wednesday

- carrot sticks with hummus dip
- sandwich with mashed banana filling
- fruit salad using grapes, dried apricots and dried mangoes
- muffin (cake-style)

Thursday

- cherry tomatoes
- 'pocket handkerchief' sandwiches with cream cheese and thinly sliced cucumber
- fromage frais
- fruit cake

Friday

- small pieces of celery spread with peanut butter
- pitta bread with grated cheese and apple
- vanilla yogurt with honey and chopped nuts if appropriate
- chocolate brownie (see page 24)

Menus for festivals and celebrations

Chinese New Year

Celebrated on the first day of the lunar calendar, usually in February. Many of the foods consumed have a symbolic meaning, either in name or shape.

- Spring rolls available at supermarket deli counters
- Chicken noodle salad (see page 27). The noodles are left uncut to symbolise a long life
- Mandarin orange. Food that is round in shape is often eaten at this time to symbolise families being complete and getting on well with each other
- Sponge cake - the word for cake sounds the same as that for tall, or high and so cake is eaten at this time to wish for success or promotion.

Mardi Gras

Literally, fat Tuesday and is celebrated with carnivals, particularly in South America on Shrove Tuesday. Traditionally pancakes are cooked, though these may not be very appetising cold in a lunchbox! Try these South American alternatives.

- Tomato salsa with tortillas (see page 26)
- South American salad (see page 26)
- Caribbean banana bread (see page 26).

Easter

Celebrated, of course, with Easter eggs. These are a symbol of the rock tomb from which Christ emerged, as well as representing new life. Think about an egg shaped menu.

- Plum cherry tomatoes
- Egg-shaped egg sandwich
- Fruit that resembles egg shapes such as red and white grapes or a kiwi that can be eaten like a boiled egg
- Chocolate crispy buns with a miniature speckled chocolate egg (see page 25).

Pesach/Passover

A spring festival, often around the same time as Easter. It represents the Jews' escape from slavery in Egypt.

- Unleavened bread, e.g. water biscuits, matzos (it needs to be unleavened because the Jews left Egypt in a hurry, before Pharaoh changed his mind)
- A hard-boiled egg (this symbolises Spring)
- Celery or parsley (either is used, to represent the bitter herbs that symbolise the bitterness of slavery)
- Flapjack or other cereal bar containing apple and walnuts (traditionally, apple and walnut paste is incorporated into the meal, representing the mortar used by Jews when they were slaves building the pyramids). See recipe for apple and walnut flapjack on page 25.

Baisakhi

An important day for Sikhs, it usually falls on 13th or 14th April and celebrates the founding of the Sikh community by Guru Gobind Singh. It also marks the start of the New Year for Sikhs in the Punjab. Try to include yellow or orange foods - a religious colour for Sikhs.

- Strips of yellow and orange peppers
- Basmati rice with fruit and nuts with a mini naan bread (see page 27)
- Papaya with lime juice.

Chinese dragon boat festival

Held on the 5th day of the 5th moon, usually in June. The festival is said to honour a poet and scholar who drowned himself when the emperor ignored his advice on how to save China. People raced in their boats to try and save him. The most famous food is zongzi - a sticky rice dumpling with a savoury filling.

- Hard boiled egg - if you balance an egg on its end at noon on this day it is said that the rest of the year will be lucky!
- Chinese salad (see page 26)
- Chinese pancakes with filling of your choice and Hoi Sin sauce
- Lychees.

Jewish New Year

Takes place in September/ October. The emphasis on honey is to represent a sweet new year!

- Couscous salad (a traditional new year food - chop tomatoes, cucumber or other salad vegetables into small pieces and add to couscous, with dressing if liked)
- Round loaves to symbolise continuity (i.e. no beginning or end). Ideally, challah bread formed into circles but any roll or round loaf would do
- Honey cake
- Apples dipped in honey (store in small pot, and cut apples into slices or rings brushed with lemon juice to prevent discolouration).

Diwali

The Hindu festival of light is celebrated in October or November. Food plays an important part in Diwali celebrations. No meat is served and sweets are made to exchange as gifts.

- Roti filled with chick pea spicy salad (see page 28). Roti are popular with vegetarian fillings. You could substitute pitta bread for roti
- Rice pudding, traditionally eaten on same plate as the rest of the meal
- Bags of cubed fruit to represent the exchange of sweets at this time.

Holi

This is a Spring festival celebrated in late February/early March. It is named after the evil goddess Holika. Images of Holika are burned to symbolise good defeating evil. It is a festival of colour and celebrates Krishna.

- Onion bhajis - a must at Holi, in preparation for unexpected guests
- Vegetable samosas (see page 27)
- Natural yogurt and honey - dairy products were Krishna's favourite food and so are served at festivals such as Holi
- Fruits of different colours for the festival of colours, such as red and white grapes and clementine segments.

Eid

Marks the end of Ramadan and is timed with the new moon, usually falling in November. Why not try some food at this time enjoyed by the Muslims of North Africa.

- Salad of cucumber, tomato, olives with a little lemon juice and olive oil
- Couscous with roasted vegetables (see page 28)
- Natural yogurt with honey
- Stoned dates - dates were eaten by the prophet Mohammed and are eaten to break the day's fast in Ramadan. They feature strongly in Eid celebrations.

Hallowe'en

On October 31st. This festival has its roots in Celtic Ireland. Spirits of the dead were said to come to earth at this time to inhabit living souls. People dressed up in scary outfits to frighten the spirits off. Turnips were originally used for lanterns but Irish emigrants in New England found that pumpkins were more plentiful.

- Pumpkin soup with bread and cheese (see page 29)
- Half apples, as described on page 10
- Small hallowe'en novelty cake.

Christmas

The celebration of the birth of Christ for Christians and a time of family celebrations for non-Christians. Add a festive Christmas-style lunchbox to the last week of the December term. This can be while the children who have school meals are eating their cooked Christmas lunch, or on another day that week so that your child can join in with the cooked meal.

- Carrot batons, raw or cooked
- Turkey roll with cranberry sauce
- Mince pie
- Satsuma
- A chocolate and a Christmas cracker.

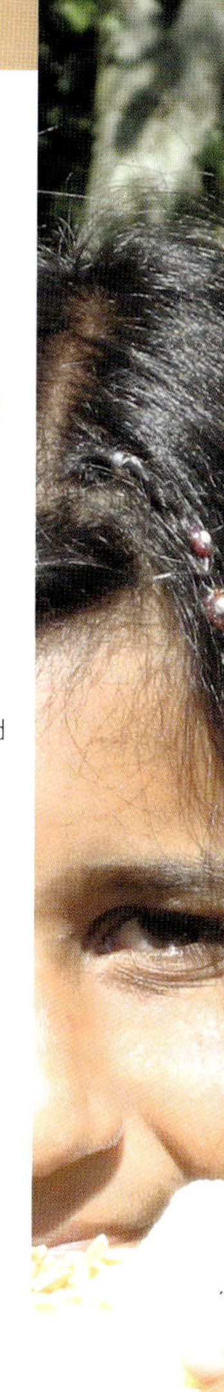
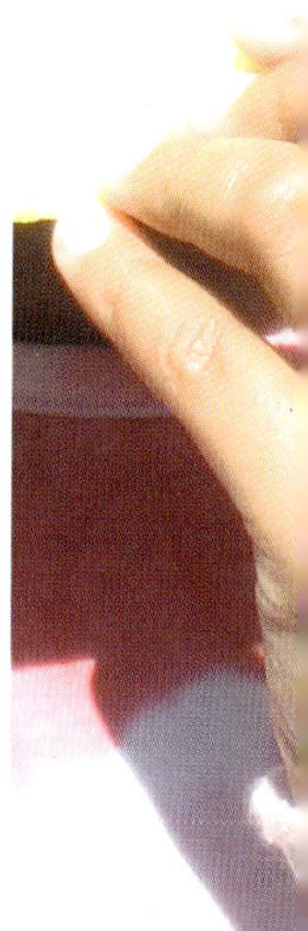

Pick and mix

If you prefer to make up your own menus, pick one item from each column. Try to include fruit and vegetables, a starchy food and a dairy product. So for example you could have cucumber sticks, tortilla wrap with grated apple and cheese, tinned fruit and a flapjack.

Starter	Starchy food (fuel food)	Filling	Dessert	Extras
Raw carrot sticks	Sandwich	Tuna and sweetcorn/cucumber/avocado	Whole fruit of your choice	Flapjack
Cucumber sticks	Bread roll	Grated apple and cheese	Fruit salad - kiwi, grapes, melon etc.	Currant bun
Celery sticks	Pitta bread	Egg and cress	Dried fruit - raisins, apricots, apples	Muffin
Peppers, sliced	Tortilla wrap	Ham and pineapple/cheese	Stewed fruit - apples, apple and pear, rhubarb	Slice of cake
Mangetout		Tinned salmon and cucumber	Tinned fruit	Fruit bread
Sugar snaps		Mashed banana	Yogurt, fruit or natural with honey/nuts	Chocolate brownie
Cherry tomatoes		Cream cheese and cucumber	Fromage frais	Cereal bar
Broccoli florets		Cheese and pickle/salad	Fruit smoothie	Carrot cake
Baby corn on the cobs		Peanut butter with or without jam		
		Sliced chicken or turkey with cranberry sauce		
With/without		Hummus and grated carrot		
Hummus		Mashed avocado		
Taramasalata		Cottage cheese		
Natural yogurt				
Cream cheese	Pasta/rice/ couscous	Tomato, ham, cheese cubes		
Mayonnaise		Ham and pineapple		
		Tuna and sweetcorn		
		Apple and cheese cubes		
		Cold roasted vegetables		
		Salmon and cucumber		
		Tuna and hard boiled egg		

Some quick and easy recipes

The recipes that follow are all suitable for preparing with your children.

Children feel proud and important when they're involved. They make a contribution to family life when they help. They may look forward to being able to show their lunchbox creations to friends and teachers.

Learning to cook is an education in itself - for adults and children - and can be rewarding and fun.

By combining a weekend cooking session with planning ahead, you can provide lunchbox solutions for the coming week. Most of the items can either be stored in airtight containers or, where appropriate, frozen and defrosted for use during the week.

Carrot soup

4 servings

1 onion
500g carrots
1 potato
900mls chicken or vegetable stock
fresh parsley, chopped

Put some olive oil in the saucepan. Add the chopped onion and carrot and cook for 5 minutes. Add the stock and parsley and simmer for 30 minutes. Puree the soup and check the seasoning.

Potato and leek soup

4 servings

500g leeks
500g potatoes
1 onion
900mls chicken or vegetable stock

Add some olive oil to a saucepan and heat. Add the chopped leeks, potatoes and onion and cook for 5 minutes. Add the stock and simmer for 30mins. Puree and check the seasoning.

Big soup

The children call this big soup because the vegetables are cut to a chunky size not pureed. This is a meal in itself and could be served in a wide necked flask.

The choice of vegetables is yours and quantities are deliberately vague as it depends on whatever needs eating up.

Approx. 5-6 servings

1 large onion
2 large carrots
1 large potato
1 large parsnip
1/4 swede
1-1 1/2 tins of tomatoes
1 tbsp tomato puree
3 large handfuls dried pasta shapes; spirals and shells work well.
3-4 leaves of spring greens

Chop all the vegetables diagonally into large chunks. Fry the onion in olive oil. Add the remaining vegetables and sweat for 10 minutes. Add the tin of tomatoes and a small amount of water if necessary. Add the dried pasta and cook until the pasta is tender, usually 30 minutes. Add the dried basil or oregano and seasoning. In the last 2-3 minutes some shredded greens can be stirred in to add colour and extra goodness.

Potato salad

Choose small salad potatoes. Either scrub or peel them and boil until just tender. Allow to cool. Mix with mayonnaise or soured cream and snip in some chives if you like.

Cheese scones

Makes 10

225g self-raising flour
2 tsp baking powder
50g grated cheese
150mls milk

Sift the flour and baking powder into a mixing bowl. Rub in the butter until the mixture resembles breadcrumbs. Stir in the cheese. Add the milk gradually, mixing all the time, until the mixture resembles a soft dough. Roll out on a floured surface to a thickness of 1cm. Cut into rounds and lightly brush the tops with milk. Place the rounds on a greased baking tray and bake at gas mark 7 / 220C for 10 minutes or until risen and browned.

Chicken Waldorf salad

Chop some cooked chicken breast, an eating apple and celery and combine with a handful of walnuts, a good squirt of lemon juice and a few raisins. Add a small amount of mayonnaise to taste.

Chocolate brownies

100g plain chocolate
100g butter
2 eggs
160g golden caster sugar
75g plain flour
1 tsp vanilla essence

Melt the chocolate with the butter and allow to cool slightly. Beat the eggs with the sugar and then beat in the chocolate mixture. Sift in the flour and beat, adding the vanilla essence.

Pour into a lined 20cm square baking tin and bake for approx. 20 - 25 minutes at gas mark 4 / 180C. Allow to cool and cut into squares. You can of course vary this recipe by adding 50g of chopped nuts.

Granny's lemon cake

200g self-raising flour
2 large eggs
125g butter or margarine
1 lemon
200g caster sugar
1/2 small cup of milk
1 tbsp hot water
pinch of salt
Pre-heat oven to gas mark 2 / 150C.

Rub the butter or margarine into the flour. Add 150g of the caster sugar. Grate in the lemon rind. In another bowl, beat together the eggs, milk and water, then add to the flour mixture. Bake in a 20cm greased cake tin for about 1 hour. Mix together the lemon juice and the remaining caster sugar, ready to pour over the cake when it comes out of the oven. Now leave to cool in its tin.

Muffins (cake-style)

These are a very versatile treat: they can be made with chocolate chips, dried fruit, fresh blueberries, bananas, grated carrot, pineapple, and so on. Here is a popular basic muffin recipe.

Makes 10 muffins.

50g butter or margarine
150g self-raising flour
50g caster sugar
1/2 tsp baking powder
1 large egg, beaten
110mls milk
125g one of the following: chocolate chips, blueberries, raspberries, sultanas or other 'buried treasure'.

Pre-heat oven to gas mark 6 / 200C. Ask your children to place 10 paper muffin cases in a muffin bun tray. Melt the butter/margarine in a saucepan over a low heat. While it cools slightly, sift the flour into a large mixing bowl and add sugar and baking powder. Mix them together. Add the milk and then the beaten egg to the melted butter/margarine, mix well, and then pour into the bowl of dry ingredients. Now mix everything together with a fork, quite quickly and roughly - a few lumps do not matter. Add the 'buried treasure' and mix it in. Divide the mixture between the muffin cases. Bake for approx. 20 minutes or until risen and golden.

Chocolate crispy buns

cornflakes
chocolate, plain or milk
raisins
mini speckled eggs

This is a goodie at Easter! The quantities are up to you; just make sure you have enough chocolate to coat all the cornflakes. Melt the chocolate in a bowl over hot water. When melted, add the cornflakes and a handful of raisins. Divide the mixture between paper cup cases and pop a miniature speckled egg on the top.

Apple and walnut flapjacks

350g porridge oats
150g brown sugar
150g butter or margarine
2 tbsp golden syrup
1 peeled and grated apple
handful of chopped nuts
1/4 tsp cinnamon (optional)
Pre-heat the oven to gas mark 4 / 180C

Melt the syrup and the butter/margarine. Add the other ingredients and stir until evenly mixed. Press into a greased baking tray and bake for about 20 minutes. Cut into squares while still hot in the tray and then leave to cool.

Chinese salad

thinly sliced Chinese leaves
handful of watercress
few mangetout
beansprouts
spring onion - chopped
dressing:
I tbsp lime juice
I tbsp oil
I tbsp light soy sauce
pinch of sugar

Mix the Chinese leaves, watercress, mangetout, beansprouts and spring onion. Combine the lime juice, oil and soy sauce in a screw topped bottle and shake to mix. Pack some chopped dry roasted peanuts to sprinkle on top if desired.

Tomato salsa

Chop a small red onion, fresh coriander and 5 medium ripe tomatoes. First blend the onion and coriander. Add the tomatoes and a touch of chilli sauce, to taste. Blend until finely chopped.

South American salad

4 servings

150g shredded white cabbage
80g cucumber diced
I mango, diced
I avocado pear, cubed
I tomato, diced
small bunch watercress
Dressing:
3tbsp freshly squeezed lime juice
3tbsp oil

Mix all the ingredients together and pack a small container of the dressing to add just before eating.

Caribbean banana bread

Makes a Ikg loaf.

275g plain flour
2 tsp baking powder
125g butter or margarine
pinch salt
100g caster sugar
2 large eggs, beaten
3 medium bananas, mashed
50g finely chopped walnuts

Pre-heat oven to gas mark 4 / 180C. Sift flour, baking powder and salt into a bowl. In a different bowl, cream together the butter/margarine and sugar until light and fluffy. Add the beaten eggs and mix quite thoroughly. Now stir in the dry ingredients and the mashed bananas, alternately, and lastly the nuts. Mix well. Pour into a greased Ikg loaf tin and bake for about one hour. Leave to cool in the tin for 10 minutes, then transfer to a wire rack. This loaf can be eaten sliced on its own or with butter.

Raita

This well known Indian dish can be varied in a number of ways and served as a dip with some raw vegetables or breadsticks. Start with natural yogurt then add one of the following combinations:

chopped cucumber and mint
chopped coriander and a pinch of nutmeg
chopped tomatoes and onion with fresh coriander

Basmati rice with fruit

2 servings

1 onion, chopped
1/2 tsp ground cumin
2 tbsp sultanas
50g chopped pineapple
1tbsp chopped dried apricots
140g rice
500mls vegetable stock
fresh coriander

Fry the onion in some olive oil with the cumin. Add the sultanas, pineapple and apricots and fry for a further 5 minutes. Add the rice and vegetable stock and bring the mixture to the boil. Simmer for 20 minutes until the rice is cooked and the liquid has been soaked up. Keep an eye on it; you may need to add a touch of water. Leave to cool and then fork in the fresh coriander.

Chicken noodle salad

4 servings

75g dry Chinese egg noodles
250g cooked chicken breast cut
into strips
80g lettuce
1 red pepper cut into strips
3 spring onions
small can of bamboo shoots, drained
Dressing:
3tbsp olive oil
2tbsp soy sauce
2 tbsp lime juice
1tsp of grated ginger

Cook the noodles as instructed on the packet. Leave to cool. Combine the chicken, lettuce, pepper, spring onions and bamboo shoots with the cold noodles.

Combine the ingredients for the dressing in a screw top container and pour onto the salad just before serving.

Vegetable samosas

1 potato chopped
1 carrot chopped
50g frozen peas
1/2 - 1 tsp mild curry paste
2 tbsp soft cheese
8 sheets filo pastry
olive oil for brushing

Boil the potato and carrot until soft. Drain and cut into small pieces. Cook the frozen peas and add to the other vegetables. Add the cheese, curry paste and season. Leave to cool. Heat the oven to gas mark 5 / 180C. Lay the pastry sheets on top of each other and cut the sheets lengthways into two strips. This means you have 16 strips altogether.

Now your children can get a production line going! Put a heaped teaspoon of the filling at the end of one strip. Fold the end of the strip of pastry diagonally across the filling, to form a triangle, then keep folding over, along the pastry strip. Repeat until all the pastry strips and filling are used up.

Place the samosas on a baking tray, and get your children to brush them lightly with olive oil and sprinkle with poppy seeds. Bake in the oven for about 15 minutes or until golden brown. Delicious either warm or cold.

Lassi

This is a traditional Indian drink and is very easy to make. Just whizz together equal quantities of natural yogurt and milk, along with ice cubes, fruit of your choice and sugar to taste. Keep cool in an insulated flask.

Chick pea spicy salad

2 servings

olive oil
1 onion, chopped
1/2 tsp mild curry paste
1/2 tsp turmeric
2 tomatoes, chopped
125g can of chick peas, drained
frozen peas
1 tbsp lemon juice
fresh coriander

Heat a small amount of olive oil in a saucepan and fry the chopped onion, curry paste and turmeric for 5 minutes. Add the chopped tomatoes, drained chick peas, frozen peas and lemon juice and cook for 10 minutes. Allow to cool and then sprinkle fresh chopped coriander on top to finish. This can be served with a naan bread or chapatti.

Couscous and roasted vegetable salad

2 servings

olive oil
1 red onion
1 red pepper, de-seeded
1 courgette
100g couscous
120mls vegetable stock
1 tomato
fresh chopped parsley

Pour some olive oil in a roasting tray and add the chopped pepper, courgette and onion. Roast in a hot oven for 30 - 40 minutes until the vegetables are browned. Allow to cool.

Meanwhile pour the stock over the couscous in a bowl and leave to stand, as per the instructions and mix. Fluff up the couscous with a fork and add the roasted vegetables, chopped tomato and parsley.

Pumpkin soup

4 servings

1 pumpkin - use the flesh of your
hollowed-out hallowe'en pumpkin
1 potato, chopped
1 onion, chopped
900mls vegetable stock
100mls crème fraiche
nutmeg (grated)

Cut the pumpkin in half and wash. Scrape out the seeds and pulp. Place the halves on an oiled baking sheet and bake, skin side up, in a hot oven until the pumpkin is tender – about 45 mins. When cool, the skin is easy to peel off and the flesh is soft.

Fry the onion and then add the chopped pumpkin and the potato. Stir in the stock and simmer until the vegetables are tender. Puree and then return to the pan and stir in the crème fraiche. Check the seasoning and finally sprinkle with some grated nutmeg.

Ready to go!

You've read the book, packed the freezer shelf and store cupboard and chatted to your child and school. Now it's time to experiment for yourself. Have fun!

Happy cooking and eating!